MW00463940

GRACE and FAITH THOUGHTS

by

ARTHUR AND CATHY MEINTJES

All scripture references in King James Version unless otherwise specified.

A KINGDOM LIFE MINISTRIES PUBLICATION
3802 Galileo Dr #C
Fort Collins, CO 80528
Tel: 970 568-8433
www.kingdomlifeministry.com
info@kingdomlifeministry.com

Published: 2008, 2011

ACKNOWLEDGEMENTS

A great BIG thank you our children Cheri, Gabby and AJ who have encouraged us to continue to pursue our hearts desire to touch the nations with the Gospel of Peace and Grace. They have unselfishly given us the opportunity to be away from home at various times. You have rejoiced with us in the good times and been a source of strength during the hard times. We love you all so much.

To Cathy's parents and Arthur's sister who have stood with us through thick and thin. Thank you for being willing to help with the kids and keep things alive and well on the home front. You are a constant source of encouragement and an awesome example of faithfulness and love.

To our home church family, thank you for your support and love. Thank you for letting us travel secure in the fact that you are all praying for us and also for being such a great part of reaching the world with grace.

To our Father God, His Son Jesus Christ and the Holy Spirit go all the glory for changing our lives and for being an eternal source of strength, power and patience while we endeavor to fulfill the call on our lives.

Arthur and Cathy Meintjes

Contents

We cannot exude self-confidence, beauty and joy without a sense of our dignity and self-worth as human beings. God has restored this dignity and self-worth completely through the finished work of Jesus Christ on the cross. He has made us accepted in the beloved. He has removed our sin and guilt. Here are some thoughts on this awesome grace we have been given.

ARTHUR and CATHY MEINTJES are the founders of KINGDOM LIFE MINISTRIES INTERNATIONAL. A revelation of the love of God and His goodness brought about a great change in their lives and ministry and their hearts' desire is to see leaders in all spheres come to an intimate and personal relationship with God. Arthur's insight into God's word and his ability to share this understanding and experience of God's love has touched many lives around the world.

One

MOSTLY WHAT GOD DOES IS LOVE YOU!

I recently watched a TV program where the scene was set at a riverside with a father and his friend watching their sons. The father looked over at his teenage son and said to his friend: "I have no say or choice in that young man's life, he has to live it his way". And the friend replied: "Yes, but you can choose what kind of father he will have." What an awesome picture of who God is! He cannot make us

6

do anything, but He has decided what kind of father He will be.

Ephesians 5:1-2 (Message Bible)
"Watch what God does, and then you do it, like children who learn proper behavior from their parents. MOSTLY WHAT GOD DOES IS LOVE YOU. Keep company with Him and learn a life of love. Observe how Christ loved us. His love was not cautious but EXTRAVAGANT. He didn't love in order to get something from us but to give everything of Himself to us. LOVE LIKE THAT!"

So many times we have been asked how we can preach so much on the love of God and whether we ever get tired of speaking about love. Our answer is an emphatic "No". We never get tired of learning about this awesome love of God.

Many people think they know all there is to know about God and love. I Corinthians 8:1-2 (Amplified) says: *"Mere knowledge causes people to be puffed up (to bear themselves loftily and be proud), but love edifies and builds up and encourages one to grow (to his full stature). If anyone imagines that he has come to know and understand much (of divine things, without love), he does not yet perceive and understand as strongly and clearly, nor has he become as intimately acquainted with anything as he ought or as is necessary."* The Bible tells me that if you say you know all things, you actually don't know much at all, because only love causes maturity to come.

Just like children learn from their parents, we need to learn from God. How do we do that? By looking at how Jesus treated people. He was the exact representation of God. Jesus always had a heart of compassion and kindness. He never ridiculed or belittled people, never called them sinners, and never took away their self-worth and dignity. In fact He always focused on how precious people were. And the Bible says that He is the same yesterday, today and forever, so we can expect Him to be the same with us today.

We need to immerse ourselves in the constant and unchanging love that God has toward us, because what He primarily does is love us. In fact that was the reason Jesus came. Because God so LOVED the world He did not want us to be separated from Him. The scripture says this love is EXTRAVAGANT which means, "going beyond what is reasonable or doing much more than is necessary." This is the Good News. We have become part of a FAMILY who has a wonderful, loving Father who has and will go to extraordinary lengths to show love to His children. In fact, Paul prays in Ephesians 3:19 (Amp) that we would come to understand and experience this love so that we can be "flooded with God Himself."

If accepting God's love in Jesus Christ was the way to get into this family, then living in that love is the only way to stay there. Many of us have tried to live in the family by keeping laws (whether Biblical or self-imposed) but sooner or later we all have to come to the realization that we cannot do it alone.

This Christian life and love is FREE. It is a gift – no payment needed! . In 2 Corinthians 3 in the Message Bible it reads: *"Nothing between us and God, our faces shining with the brightness of his face."* Decide today to take it and live your life totally and utterly reliant on God and His love. It is the only sure foundation.

Two

THE POWER OF LOVE

In Acts 2:8 Jesus told the disciples to wait until they received the Holy Ghost who would give them power (ability, efficiency and might) (AMP) to be *witnesses* to the ends of the earth. They would take the word of salvation and wholeness to nations.

I believe the Holy Ghost was sent so we could be witnesses to the *power of God's love* toward man, his ultimate creation. Unfortunately today, many people put so much focus on the *love of power* that they forget about the *power of love*. Jesus never intended for us to focus on the "power" or the spectacular that so many thrive on. He wanted us to realize that it is because of God's unending passion for mankind that we witness the supernatural.

The gospel is the power of this love working together with the Holy Ghost to lead people into sozo (salvation and wholeness in every sense of the word). *The gospel is the good news message of the finished work of the cross of Jesus Christ and everything it accomplished for ALL men for ALL time because of the free gift of the grace, goodness, mercy, love and forgiveness of God.*

I am reminded of a part in the Iron Man II movie where the main character is watching a video recorded before his father died. The young man had always believed he wasn't good enough and couldn't meet his father's expectations and was a failure, but his father tells him via the recording that he is and always has been his father's GREATEST CREATION. This is such a picture of mankind today. Too many people feel they have failed God and don't measure up. The gospel is the good news that YOU ARE AND ALWAYS HAVE BEEN GOD'S GREATEST CREATION and because of that the cosmos was created and He has done everything needed for your salvation!

The whole salvation plan depended on God's agape love for mankind. My favorite definition of agape love is that **in**

my worst hour God sees me as precious, valuable and to be highly esteemed. God who knows ALL things doesn't give a thought to who we are in our worst moment but loves us with all the agape that He is. God IS love and that love springs FROM God. *"Beloved, let us love one another: for love is of God; and every one that loveth is born of God, and knoweth God. He that loveth not knoweth not God; for God is love* (I John 4:7-8). Love is who God is, not something He possesses. He cannot be separated from it, ever.

When we understand and receive this love, we receive HIM. Love is brought to completion and perfection through our union with Christ because of God's love for us. *And we have known and believed the love that God hath to us. God is love; and he that dwelleth in love dwelleth in God, and God in him. Herein is our love made perfect, that we may have boldness in the day of judgment: because as he is, so are we in this world.* (I Jn 4:16-17)

If we don't keep the love of God for mankind first place in every Bible conversation, we will end up arguing about pointless things. We can only help others if we keep the ***power of the love of God*** in the forefront of our hearts and minds. Once we open our eyes and hearts to the ***power of love*** it is almost impossible to misinterpret God's Word. *"Whereas the object and purpose of our instruction and charge is LOVE, which springs from a pure heart and a good (clear) conscience and sincere (unfeigned) faith."* (I Tim 1:5)

I Corinthians 13 is an awesome discovery of God's love for mankind and we will discuss it in depth later, but I Corinthians 14:1 goes on to read: **"Go after (this) love as if your life depended on it – because it does" (MSG)**. We need to know God's love as much as we need each breath of air. Nothing that life can throw at us can change or remove the power of this love (Romans 8:35-39)

Jude 21 reminds us to stay in the boundaries where the love of God can reach and keep us (TLB). The only way to 'get out' of this awesome love is to believe the lies of the enemy and daily life and that is through our own thoughts and perceptions of life. Our circumstances NEVER change God's love for us! We cannot allow the circumstances of life to draw us out of the awareness of this love. *"God so loved the world that He gave His son so we would be safe and sound in Him. "*(John 3:16) AMP

Jesus provided safety: The provision of security and protection, free from the feelings of risk or danger.

And soundness: A state of being healthy, whole or complete. Not diseased, damaged or inferior.

You are ALWAYS safe and sound in the *power of love*. No matter what life throws at you or how you feel about life, the *power of love* will keep you safe, and make you whole. It will NEVER fail you!

Three

THE OFFSPRING OF GOD
Our True Identity

For as he (a man) thinks in his heart, so is he…!" – Proverbs 23:7

Keep and guard your heart with all vigilance and above all that you guard, for out of it flow the springs of life." - Proverbs 4:23 AMP

According to these scriptures it is self-evident that the outcome and success of our life and our relationships is determined by what we deeply believe in our hearts especially what we believe about God, about ourselves and about others!

Identity the Key

Almost all of the limitations we experience in leadership, relationship and life in general are as a result of our sense of identity, or the lack thereof. We can only ever be, and achieve what is consistent with our belief system and who we believe we truly are! The truth of the matter is that the failure or success of our life, and relationships depends on our deep down identity or belief of who we really are. A strong and healthy identity is the key to being an effective leader, and having stable and healthy relationships.

A question I am frequently asked by pastors and ministers is: *Can the gospel of grace and peace alone influence people to the point of changing the way they see and feel about themselves, and as a result change the way they relate to other people around them?*

The Answer is: Absolutely!

The Gospel is Unique

There are a great many claims in the Gospel of Jesus Christ that sets Christianity apart from all other major religions of the world and makes our faith unique!! One of the most important claims is that it declares that God through the work of Jesus Christ has done everything necessary to produce the results needed for our total inclusion in the identity of His son Jesus Christ!

Identity in Christ our Rock!

About two years ago God started speaking to me about seeing and finding my origin and identity in Him as the Rock that gave me birth! The passage of scripture that the Lord used was from Deuteronomy 32, a prophetic Psalm of Moses. In this Psalm Moses describes God as "the Rock". *"...ascribe ye greatness unto our God. He is the Rock, his work is perfect: for all his ways are judgment: a God of truth and without iniquity, just and right is he.* Deut 32:3 - 4 [KJV]

Right through the Bible we find references to God and more specifically of Jesus as the Rock. Moses uses this as a description for God because a rock speaks of strength, dependability, durability, stability, steadfastness, and security.

We see God described as:

> The rock of our Salvation!
> The rock of our Strength!
> The rock of our Refuge!
> The bedrock of our Faith, and
> The rock of ages!

So it is easy for us to identify with God as "the Rock" and we are able to relate to Him as having all these attributes described above.

Deuteronomy 32 verse 18, "*... Of the Rock that begat thee thou art unmindful, and hast forgotten God that formed thee.*"

My first thought was that God was drawing my attention to the fact that I had been unmindful of Him, and that I had forgotten Him, just as the people of Israel had done those many years ago! But the

Lord very quickly assured me that even though it might be true that in many ways I have been unmindful of Him, and many times I have forgotten Him this was not what He was drawing my attention to! He was showing me that even though it is true that we have often forgotten Him and are unmindful of God the "Rock" that gave us birth, He "the Rock" (who is always the same) has never forgotten about us!

This is the message of the Gospel of Jesus Christ! God refuses to be unmindful of man, and He has never forgotten us! This is what God wants the world to know. That even though they might have forgotten the Rock of their birth, the Rock has never forgotten them!

So many people want to "find" God by fasting, prayer and an almost never-ending series of do's and dont's but listen to what Isaiah 51: 1 says! *"Listen to me, you that pursue righteousness, you that seek the LORD. Look to the rock from which you were hewn, and to the quarry from which you were dug." Is 51:1 (NRSV)*

Are you pursuing righteousness? Are you seeking the Lord? Then this scripture says very simply "look" to the Rock from which you were hewn. This is not hard or difficult; looking is a very easy and an effortless thing to do! To pursue righteousness, and to seek after the Lord is to look to God or more importantly to Jesus, for an example, for our identification. If we understand the context of the verse correctly we also find the source of our origin. This is what I believe Peter saw in his revelation of Jesus in Matt 16!

Peter's Revelation

This is the account of Jesus asking his disciples who men said he was, *Matt 16:13-16 "When Jesus came into the coasts of Caesarea Philippi, he asked his disciples, saying, Whom do men say that I the Son of man am? And they said, Some say that thou art John the Baptist: some, Elias; and others, Jeremias, or one of the prophets. He saith unto them, But whom say ye that I am? And Simon Peter answered and said, Thou art the Christ, the Son of the living God." KJV*

Although other people said that they thought that Jesus was one of the various prophets, Simon's answer was: "You are the Christ, the Son of the living God." So in essence the revelation that Simon got was that Jesus is "The Christ" and that his "origin is of God!" Matt 16:17 *And Jesus answered and said unto him, Blessed art thou, Simon Barjona: for flesh and blood hath not revealed it unto thee, but my Father which is in heaven.*

So when Jesus replies to Simon here, He refers to his (Simon's) natural birth or origin, *"Simon Barjona or Simon son of Jona"*, and He goes on to say, *"flesh and blood hath not revealed it unto thee, but my Father which is in heaven."*

Essentially Jesus is saying to Simon that his fleshly birth, genealogy or origin cannot reveal this truth that he had just seen. Only God can!

Then Jesus says to Simon, *18 And I say also unto thee, That thou art Peter (petros), and upon this rock (petra) I will build my church; and the gates of hell shall not prevail against it.* When He says, *"I say also unto thee"* in the English it sounds like He is just saying "I say to you" but the word "also" in the Greek adds a far deeper meaning! In the original language Jesus is saying; *"...and I say also or "likewise" unto you Simon as you have just said unto me!"* What I believe Jesus was saying to Peter is: "I say likewise back to you Simon (what you have just said to me I now say back to you) you also are "Petros", Greek for "...a piece of rock, or fragment of rock", *"Petros" hewn from the Rock "Petra"*

Jesus is showing Simon, that the revelation he had of Jesus and His origin is also a revelation of his (Peter's) own origin. He is cut from the same rock, and has his origin in the living God just like Jesus. Then He says; *"…upon this Rock "Petra" I will build, put together, construct and confirm my church!"*

There is nothing that can establish, complete and distinguish a person better, than a revelation of his true identity and origin as it is revealed in the person of Christ. Church is to be the place where people discover their true origin in God, and find their true identity in Christ.

This reminds me of a true story I heard from a good friend, Francois du Toit. In the 1980's in Africa the fish eagle was an endangered species and everything possible was being done to try and rescue these birds from extinction. A Nature Conservation organization in South Africa was given a fish eagle that had been in captivity for more than 10 years and had never learned to fly. Their intention was to reintroduce this bird to the wild and their excitement was at an all time high the day that they were finally going to open the cage and release the bird to soar free.

To their amazement the bird did not take off in flight, but instead only sat on a rock as if still captive in a cage. Later that afternoon after they had given up on trying everything to get this bird to take off in flight and discover its new freedom, a wild fish eagle came over the mountain and started to call out with its own very distinct call that can be heard from long distances. Something very interesting happened.

The previously captive eagle's eyes lit up. The second time the wild eagle called out, the captive eagle started looking around with great excitement and when the wild eagle called out for the third time the once captive bird took off in flight and it was not long before he was soaring with the wild eagles.

Something awakened in that bird, when he discovered who he really was. He was for all intents and purposes born from above or born again! Nobody had to instruct him on how to fly because it was in his genes. He was an eagle that was made to fly and soar on the winds!

This also is true about every one of us, when we will discover our true origin and identity in the rock who gave us birth.

We are born from above or born again!

When writing to the church at Colossae, Paul gave us some profound insight. *"Be careful that nobody spoils your faith through intellectualism or high-sounding nonsense. Such stuff is at best founded on men's ideas of the nature of the world and disregards Christ! Yet it is in Him that God gives a full and complete expression of Himself in bodily form. Moreover, your own completeness is realized in Him, who is the ruler over all authorities and the supreme head over all power.* Col 2: 8 – 10 JB Phillips

Firstly, Paul says that, *"in Him (Jesus) God gives a full and complete expression of Himself in bodily form.**"** He explains that in Jesus Christ, God has fully expressed himself in a bodily or human form. So if we saw Jesus we would see a man fully expressing who God is.

Secondly, Paul says, *"Moreover (or more importantly!) your own completeness is realized in Him"*. So Paul is saying that in Jesus is the full expression of God in the flesh, but when we look at him we also see who we are! **We are the offspring of God!**

God's Assurance

Most people read the bible and relate to the Gospel of Jesus Christ. They read it, hear it and receive it as good news, but many still feel like it will never really work for them, because they fail to see themselves as the offspring of God.

One of the boldest claims of the Gospel of Jesus Christ is that not only does every believer have salvation, redemption and forgiveness, but every believer has been given the right and the privilege to be the offspring of the living God. (John 1:12-13) [AMP] *But to as many as did receive and welcome Him, He gave the authority (power, privilege, right) to become the children of God, that is, to those who believe in (adhere to, trust in, and rely on) His name — [Is 56:5.] Who owe their birth neither to bloods nor to the will of the flesh [that of physical impulse] nor to the will of man [that of a natural father], but to God. [They are born of God!]"*

So many believers still suffer under a heavy burden of guilt, condemnation and rejection because of the circumstances of their birth. Many have been born into this world as a result of the sins of their parents. Maybe they were illegitimate children, because of adultery, or because of prostitution. Others might even be the product of incest. Some people were born in circumstances where they might have been given up for adoption or ended up in an orphanage. As a result they feel like outcasts. Others live with the torment of rejection, and for many, life is almost not worth living!

But here in verse 13, Jesus explains to us who it is that we owe our birth to! We owe our birth neither to being from pure blood, nor to the will of man or that of a natural father, but to God! You are born of God!

You are the offspring of God Himself!

Wow what a powerful truth!

No matter what the circumstances of your birth, you have the assurance of God that none of that really matters. Because you owe your birth to none of these things or circumstances, but to God as your only true and real Father.

Four

DRINKING FROM THE WELL

"You have to go to this meeting Arthur! God is moving in a powerful way! This is just what you need. It was a lifesaver for me. My life had been so dry and meaningless lately but now I have a new lease on life".

These were the words of a good friend of mine. We have known each other for many years now, and I realized that he was dead serious about this special meeting at his church.

There have been so many of these special meetings, all of which promised that it would be the answer to what was lacking in my life. Only to find that a couple of days after these meetings when everything was back to normal, the kids were back at school, the phone was ringing at the office, the bills needed paying and the beggar at my door was looking at me for some hand-out or money, that there was still a void and a lack in my heart.

But today, I just did not have the same desire and need to go to yet another special meeting. I did not know how to tell Paul that I just did not need to go to these meetings any more. At first I thought that I must be very backslidden and spiritually numb. Guilt and shame started to well up in my heart, because it is generally accepted in Christian circles that if you are a serious and committed Christian (which I considered myself to be) then you should have a continuous desire and need for meetings like these.

Finally I made some excuses for why I would not be able to go with him to the meeting and went home. I started to think about what had just taken place, and I asked the Lord to help me because I did not want to be insensitive to the things of God. I wanted the Lord to show me if there was anything amiss in my relationship with Him. Why was it that I do not have that desire and deep need anymore? The Lord led me to read a passage of scripture that was very familiar to me.

(John 4: 7 – 14) *There cometh a woman of Samaria to draw water: Jesus saith unto her, Give me to drink. (For his disciples were gone away unto the city to buy meat.) Then saith the woman of Samaria unto him, How is it that thou, being a Jew, askest drink of me, which am a woman of Samaria? for the Jews have no dealings with the Samaritans. Jesus answered and said unto her, If thou knewest the gift of God, and who it is that saith to thee, Give me to drink; thou wouldest have asked of him, and he would have given thee living water. The woman saith unto him, Sir, thou hast nothing to draw with, and the well is deep: from whence then hast thou that living water? Art thou greater than our father Jacob, which gave us the well, and drank thereof himself, and his children, and his cattle? Jesus answered and said unto her,*

Whosoever drinketh of this water shall thirst again: But whosoever drinketh of the water that I shall give him shall never thirst; but the water that I shall give him shall be in him a well of water springing up into everlasting life. The woman saith unto him, Sir, give me this water, that I thirst not, neither come hither to draw."

In these seven verses I found one of the most liberating truths I have ever seen. Jesus was asking for a drink of water from a woman from Samaria. She was surprised that Jesus being a Jew would ask her for anything. Then Jesus said something even more surprising, *"If thou knewest the gift of God, and who it is that saith to thee, Give me to drink; thou wouldest have asked of him, and he would have given thee living water."* I'm sure she must have looked around to see where Jesus was hiding His rope and pail to draw the water out of the well. When she was fully satisfied that he did not have one, she said *"Sir, thou hast nothing to draw with, and the well is deep: from whence then hast thou that living water?"*

Jesus, taking this opportunity to teach her as well us a very important reality said, *"Whosoever drinketh of this water shall thirst again: But whosoever drinketh of the water that I shall give him shall never thirst; but the water that I shall give him shall be in him a well of water springing up into everlasting life."*

Whenever water is mentioned in the word of God it is always a symbol of life.

Jesus was making it very clear that there are two sources that we can derive or get life from.

We can go to all the places or (wells) that this world has to offer. It may be all the places and things that lust, perversion, and the appetites of the flesh have to offer. It may be all the things and places that knowledge and worldly wisdom has to offer, or it might even be all the things and rewards that religion has to offer.

But Jesus said, *"Whosoever drinketh of this water shall thirst again:"* I believe that Jesus is saying that although many of these things and places can give you temporary relief, and even give you some form of life, it cannot satisfy the deep need and thirst in the human heart. Even many of us go through life drinking at the wells of what this world can give us. We get involved with religious activities and many other so called spiritual things that can only satisfy us for short periods. Thus we find Christians running from one place to another, from one meeting to another, and from one person to another looking for that life or significance of life only a meaningful, intimate relationship with God can give us.

Secondly Jesus said, *"But whosoever drinketh of the water that I shall give him shall never thirst; but the water that I shall give him shall be in him a well of water springing up into everlasting life."*

Jesus says there is another source of life, and that source of life is the living water that He has come to give us. If we will drink from this water, or let me put it another way, if we will partake of that which He has come to give us, we will never thirst again. Because within us will spring up a well of life that will sustain us, and we will never have to look any were else for significance of life again.

Jesus came to give us life (Zoë) the life of God, the life that sustains God right now. (John 10:10) That life is a self - existent life that is born out of faith righteousness before God that enables us to have an unbroken, uninterrupted meaningful relationship with God the Father: a relationship where we never have to feel unworthy, unaccepted or unlovable again. This is the meaning of life, this is significance, and this is what every person in the world wants and needs, but this is what can never be found in any other place, person or "well" that this world can offer us.

Unless we start believing fully in the finished work of Jesus we will always thirst. The work of Jesus on the cross and faith and that work alone gives me access to an intimate and personal relationship with Almighty God who is also my Father. This is what Jesus said in John 17: 3 *"And this is eternal life: [it means] to know (to perceive, recognize, become acquainted with, and understand) You, the only true and real God, and [likewise] to know Him, Jesus [as the] Christ (the Anointed One, the Messiah), Whom You have sent."* AMP

I realized that day, that the absence of the desire and need was not the result of me being backslidden or unspiritual but in fact I had become fulfilled and satisfied in a meaningful and intimate relationship with my Father. I did not need another meeting, or person to give me significance of life.

That does not mean that special meetings are wrong, or redundant. I still attend special meetings and I still listen to men of God preaching the Word, but I do not need it for life anymore. I have a well of living water (Zoe) life within me so that I will never thirst again.

Five

SAFE AND SOUND THROUGH HIM

The gospel of Jesus Christ is just so awesome and full of revelation concerning the good intent of God towards man. It never ceases to me amaze how profoundly simple it really is. Right from the beginning God's intent for mankind has been to make us safe and sound through Jesus Christ. In the beginning God made man and placed him in the garden. A place where man would be safe and sound having everything they would ever need. In the midst of this garden He also put the tree of life (Jesus) and His intent was that man would choose to eat of the tree of life and forever be made safe and sound through Him.

We all know the unfortunate outcome of that story. Man chose to be a law unto himself and decided to eat of the tree of the knowledge of good and evil, thereby determining his own safety and soundness deciding for himself what is good or evil. Ever since then man has tried to work out his own safety and soundness without much success, always desperately looking and searching for the missing secret to life. For the most part he has lived life without confidence, hope and peace.

In the gospel of John, Jesus once again makes God's intent clear when He speaks to Nicodemus in (John 3: 9 – 17). Even after Jesus explains the new birth to him, Nicodemus is still not clear about the eternal intent of God towards mankind. In verse 10 Jesus is amazed that Nicodemus does not understand God's eternal intent for man. John 3:10 *"Jesus replied, Are you the teacher of Israel, and yet do not know nor understand these things? [Are they strange to you?]"* [AMP]

To any man that is still trying to work out his safety and soundness on his own, the words of Jesus are strange and hard to understand even today. So Jesus made it clear by saying (John 3:14-17) *And just as Moses lifted up the serpent in the desert [on a pole], so must [so it is necessary that] the*

Son of Man be lifted up [on the cross], [Num 21:9.] In order that everyone who believes in Him [who cleaves to Him, trusts Him, and relies on Him] may not perish, but have eternal life and [actually] live forever! For God so greatly loved and dearly prized the world that He [even] gave up His only begotten (unique) Son, so that whoever believes in (trusts in, clings to, relies on) Him shall not perish (come to destruction, be lost) but have eternal (everlasting) life. For God did not send the Son into the world in order to judge (to reject, to condemn, to pass sentence on) the world, but that the world might find salvation and be made safe and sound through Him. [AMP]

It is so important for us to understand and believe this Gospel, this good news. Paul's understanding and proclamation of the Gospel was that it was a mystery. He said that the Gospel or the good news of Jesus Christ is a truth that was hidden [mystery] from the very beginning, but now in the New Testament it has been revealed. (Col 1:26-27) *This message has kept secret for centuries and generations past, but now it has been revealed to his own holy people. For it has pleased God to tell his people that the riches and glory of Christ are for you Gentiles, too. For this is the secret: Christ lives in you, and this is your assurance that you will share in his glory. [NLT]*

This is the mystery, or the secret, "Christ in you the hope of glory." This mystery reveals something so awesome and powerful that many people have a hard time seeing it and believing it. It reveals the fact that when we believe in Jesus Christ as our savior and our righteousness, we are intimately inseparable from Christ. Even John in his first epistle says, (1 John 4:15-17) *Whosoever shall confess that Jesus is the Son of God, God dwelleth in him, and he in God. [Intimately inseparable] And we have known and believed the love that God hath to us. God is love; and he that dwelleth in love dwelleth in God, and God in him. Herein is our love made perfect, that we may have boldness in the day of judgment: because as he is, so are we in this world.* KJV

"As He is so are we in this world." There it is in a nutshell so to speak. It is so simple but yet so hard to perceive. That as Jesus is now at the right hand of God the Father totally accepted, loved and unashamed is exactly how we are in this world before God. This means that we are just as right with God as Jesus is at this very moment in time. Just think about it, is Jesus sick today? No! Then just as He is today, so are you and I in this world today. Is God angry with Jesus today? No! Then just as He is, so are we in this world today. You might even ask yourself the question, is God disappointed with Jesus today? No! Then God is not disappointed in you today. We are intimately inseparable from Jesus in the new birth. Therefore Paul says in (2 Cor 1:20) *"For no matter how many promises God has made, they are "Yes" in Christ.* (NIV)

In Jesus all the promises of God are yes to us, we are qualified to receive all and every one of God's promises just because we are intimately inseparable from Him when we believe.

What is even more powerful and profound is that this can never change, nothing we do or say can change God's mind about us no matter what. Paul makes it even more clear in the second letter of Timothy (2 Tim 2:11-13) *The saying is sure and worthy of confidence: If we have died with Him, we shall also live with Him. Notes that Paul says that this truth of being intimately inseparable from Jesus is sure and worthy of confidence. We can be sure and confident that this is true and established forever. Then he goes on, "If we endure, we shall also reign with Him. If we deny and disown and reject Him, He will also deny and disown and reject us. If we are faithless [do not believe and are untrue to Him], He remains true (faithful to His Word and His righteous character), for He cannot deny Himself.* [AMP]

If we read this without going a little further into it we will come away from this verse believing that we are not very safe and sound in our relationship with Jesus. But just the opposite is true.

When we look at the word "deny" used here in this verse, we see that if we take it the way it is directly translated it changes the whole meaning and understanding of the passage of scripture.

DENY: arneomai means: (a) "to say... Not; or to contradict," e.g., Mark 14:70; John 1:20; 18:25,27; 1 John 2:22; (from Vine's Expository Dictionary of Biblical Words, Copyright (c)1985, Thomas Nelson Publishers)

Deny here means to "say...not", or to "contradict."

Paul says that if we contradict God, or say something about Him or about ourselves that is not in agreement with the truth of the finished work of Jesus on the cross then God will contradict us and He will have to speak the truth. If we start doubting (If we are faithless) that God's will is to make us safe and sound through Jesus, He remains true (faithful to His Word and His righteous character). He cannot deny Himself. He remains faithful to His covenant and His word, for He cannot change. God can only declare what is already true about you and what He has done.

This means that WE might change our minds about Him, but He will never change His mind about US, no matter what. We are safe and sound through Him. Let this give you confidence today to believe God for every promise you will ever need to be fulfilled in your life.

Six

GUILT FREE LIVING
Serving God with Pure Motives

For so many Christians all they have ever known and believed about God, and the Bible has been rooted in guilt, condemnation and fear, which has produced motives that are mostly inferior and has rendered their Christian lives to be difficult, unfulfilling and unproductive. This in turn only produces further emotions of indebtedness, obligation, and the fear of judgment and punishment. They start to develop a mentality of performance and the desire for reward, which induces feelings of inferiority, a low sense of self- worth, depression, isolation and rejection.

The definition for "GUILT" is very much the same as "Judgment". It means to be under sentence; condemnation or brought to trial, or justice. The dictionary defines the word "GUILT" as a "feeling of responsibility or remorse for some offense, crime or wrong, etc whether real or imagined"

As Christians our guilt goes even further and is rooted in the perceived belief of having offended a holy, and righteous God. This issue of guilt is as old as man himself. The root of guilt goes as far back as the first people on the earth. Adam and Eve were the first to experience the problem of guilt after they ate the fruit of the tree that God specifically told them not to eat. Guilt has been part of man's psychological and emotional makeup ever since.

There is no emotion that is more destructive than the emotion of guilt, because at its root, guilt is the condition of being condemned and separated from a holy God and deserving of divine judgment and punishment. Constant guilt in a believer's life is not conducive to emotional wellbeing and victorious Christian living. Yet these are the very emotions many Christians live with all their lives. They believe it is normal to be weighed down with guilt, condemnation and fear, and many believe this kind of guilt to actually be a Christian emotion!

Statistics in the past have shown that pentecostals, charismatics, and full-gospel people, suffer with guilt and guilt related emotional disorders more than any other religious group in the world. Depression and related social disorders have reached epidemic proportions in our western world. For the majority of believers their emotions are so deeply rooted in guilt and condemnation that it becomes almost impossible for them to correctly respond to their daily relationship with God.

Let me explain what I mean. Most of us have loved ones that we enjoy spending time with. What would the correct emotional response be for any person who was not able to be with a loved one for a prolonged period of time? I believe that the correct emotional response would be a sense of longing, and missing our loved ones, wanting to be with them and spend time with them. I spend a great deal of time away from my wife and family and I know the deep longing and feelings of missing them when I am away. I sometimes get to a place were all I want is to just be able to smell my wife, I long just to be able to smell her perfume.

Well we say that we love God and have a loving relationship with Him. What is the prevailing emotion most believers have when they fail to have a quiet or personal time with God for a prolonged period of time? I would venture to say that for most it would be guilt, condemnation, fear and a sense of failure. If we are really honest with ourselves I'm sure we will admit that none of us can claim that we are entirely free from the influence of this kind of guilt in our Christian lives. All of us in some way or another are either partially or wholly motivated by this hidden guilt.

Guilt has its roots in self-righteousness

The religious system that most of us have grown up with makes it almost impossible to live free from this kind of guilt. Most of what the church believes about God and the Bible makes it almost impossible for people to live in the freedom and liberty that Jesus came to give. Many believers are totally entangled in religious legalistic self-righteousness, a toxic mixture of Old Testament law, or self-effort and New Testament hope. It is in this religious system that is entrenched in the church today, where all guilt has its root.

In Rom 3: 19 Paul gives us a clear understanding about what happens to anyone who lives his or her Christian life under the Law, or in works-righteousness and self-effort.

"Now we know that what things soever the law saith, it saith to them who are under the law: that every mouth may be stopped, and all the world may become guilty before God." (KJV) Rom 3:19

Paul makes it very clear that the emotion of guilt is the direct result of living under the law, or in self-effort or works-righteousness. So guilt is one of the most self-righteous feelings or emotions that any believer can experience. When there is guilt in our lives it is a strong indication that we are under law and that we are living legalistic and self-righteous.

Now I know that many Christians wonder how they will ever be motivated if they don't feel guilty, or if guilt does not play a significant part in their relationship with God. When you take away guilt motivation, many Christians are suddenly lost and don't know how to follow Jesus. In many circles today guilt is seen as a means of overcoming the problems, or the sins we have in our lives. In reality whatever you still feel guilty about, continues to have power over your life. It will bind you to the very thing you feel guilty about.

Guilt free living

Guilt free living is exactly what God wants for us as men and women of God. Freedom from guilt is at the very heart of God's plan for man, through the finished work of Jesus Christ.

Luke 4:17-19   *"And there was delivered unto him the book of the prophet Esaias. And when he had opened the book, he found the place where it was written, The Spirit of the Lord is upon me, because he hath anointed me to preach the gospel to the poor; he hath sent me to heal the brokenhearted, to preach deliverance to the captives, and recovering of sight to the blind, to set at liberty them that are bruised, To preach the acceptable year of the Lord." (KJV)*

In this passage of scripture Jesus quotes from Isaiah 61: 1 – 3 and He proclaims the year of jubilee when all debts are cancelled, all slaves are freed, and all property is returned to the original owners. Jesus makes it clear that not only is His ministry to set us free from sin, but also to cleanse us from a sense of indebtedness and guilt. See what the writer of Hebrews says about this in chapter one and verse three in the Amplified Bible.

"...When He had by offering Himself accomplished our cleansing of sins and riddance of guilt, He sat down at the right hand of the divine Majesty on high,"

Jesus not only cleansed us of our sins, but also rid us of the guilt that came with the sin. There are multitudes of reasons why people live with the crippling affects of guilt in their lives. Some live with false guilt. This is the guilt that we put on each other in order to manipulate one another. Some live with real guilt. This is the guilt that haunts us because of the times in our lives when we have violated our conscience through things we have seen, or things that we have allowed ourselves to do. And then some people live with tremendous shame because of abusive relationships, or because of sexual abuse. I want to tell you today, that no matter what the source of your guilt is, God's will is for you to live guilt free.

Guilt of the Past

One of the greatest sources of guilt, condemnation and emotional distress in our lives is the failures, mistakes, sins, indiscretions and weaknesses of the past.

For many, their future progress and happiness has been postponed or [put on hold] because of the guilt of the past. This does not need to be the case at all. In Jesus Christ, your future does not have to be determined by your past. According to the New Covenant truth of the finished work of the cross, our whole future is determined by and through the life and the work of someone else, namely Jesus Christ of Nazareth. After all the Gospel of Jesus Christ is not about your past, it is about your future.

(II Cor 5: 17 – 21) JB Phillips

"For if a man is in Christ he becomes a new person altogether – the Past is finished and gone, everything has become fresh and new. ... God was in Christ personally reconciling the World to Himself – not counting their sins against

them – and has commissioned us with the message of reconciliation."

All my past, "good or bad," is finished and gone, all my sin, all my failures, all my indiscretions, and all my guilt of the past is gone.

Behold the Lamb of God

Under the Old Covenant when a man sinned, he could have his sins taken care of by taking a lamb to be sacrificed at the temple. The Priest, representing God, would examine and scrutinize the Lamb to find something wrong with it. He would never examine or scrutinize the man to find something wrong with him. When the lamb had been examined and the priest was satisfied that it was spotless and pure, it would be sacrificed in place of the man to pay for the sin of the man who was guilty, and he would go free.

In John chapter one and in verse twenty-nine Jesus is referred to as the Lamb of God.

29 The next day John saw Jesus coming to him and said, Look! There is the Lamb of God, Who takes away the sin of the world! [AMP] John 1:29

In Luke 23:4-25 we find Pilate and Herod, the highest authorities of the day examining Jesus the Lamb of God. In verse 22 Pilate declares Jesus to be spotless, without a cause of death in Him.

Vs 22. "And he said unto them the third time, Why, what evil hath he done? I have found no cause of death in him: I will therefore chastise him, and let him go."

Even so, Jesus is executed in place of the man who was put in prison for sedition and murder, giving us a wonderful picture of the great exchange. Because of Jesus, the Lamb of God, we can now live our lives free from sin and the penalty of that sin, knowing that sin is no longer an issue between us and God, living free from guilt, condemnation and fear. Jesus truly is the Lamb of God who takes away the sin of the world.

The problem that we have in the heart of so many believers today is that we see and admit or agree to this statement that John the Baptist made here in John 1: 29.

But in reality we do not believe and live our lives as believers according to this truth, because when we still live with a guilty, evil conscience toward God. It means that we do not acknowledge Jesus Christ's sacrifice of propitiation!

The question that we need to ask ourselves is this: Did Jesus take away the sin of the world in and through His sacrifice of propitiation or not?

The answer to this question is made clear to us through the many writings of Paul and John and also the writer of the book of Hebrews. So let us now look at some of these verses and see if that bears out in scripture.

In first John 2: 1-2, the apostle John writes: *MY LITTLE children, I write you these things so that you may not violate God's law and sin. But if anyone should sin, we have an Advocate (One Who will intercede for us) with the Father – [it is] Jesus Christ [the all] righteous [upright, just, Who conforms to the Father's will in every purpose, thought, and action].*

2 And He [that same Jesus Himself] is the propitiation (the atoning sacrifice) for our sins, and not for ours alone but also for [the sins of] the whole world. [AMP]

The word propitiation used here literally talks about the satisfying of the perfect justice of a holy and righteous God. Thereby making it possible for God to show complete mercy without compromising the righteousness of His justice. So John writes that Jesus Himself is the propitiation *(the satisfying of the perfect justice of a holy and righteous God*) for our sin, and not just for our sin but the sin of the whole world. According to John Jesus took away the sin of the whole world!!

In first John 4: 9-10, John is proclaims the extent of God's love and writes: *Vs 9 In this the love of God was made manifest (displayed) where we are concerned: in that God sent His Son, the only begotten or unique [Son], into the world so that we might live through Him.*

10 In this is love: not that we loved God, but that He loved us and sent His Son to be the propitiation (the atoning sacrifice) for our sins. [AMP]

Again John uses this word propitiation, declaring the fact that the sacrifice of Jesus Christ has taken care of the sin problem between man and God.

In the book of Romans the apostle Paul writes: *Vs 23. Since all have sinned and are falling short of the honor and glory which God bestows and receives.* Romans 3: 23

Unfortunately most of the time people only read this verse and stop, leaving out the next couple of verses, leaving us without any hope. Paul uses this statement in verse 23 as a contrast to highlight the next two verses. Therefore, these verses need to be read and interpreted together.

24[All] are justified and made upright and in right standing with God, freely and gratuitously by His grace (His unmerited favor and mercy), through the redemption which is [provided] in Christ Jesus,

25 Whom God put forward [before the eyes of

all] as a mercy seat and propitiation by His blood [the cleansing and life-giving sacrifice of atonement and reconciliation, to be received] through faith. This was to show God's righteousness, because in His divine forbearance He had passed over and ignored former sins without punishment. [AMP]

Notice that the Amplified Bible helps us to see that we cannot just quote or use verse 23 by itself, because verse 24 also starts with the word **"All".** In verse 23 "All have sinned" but in verse 24 "All are justified" through the redemption that is in Christ Jesus. Then in verse 25 Paul tells us how God did this. By Jesus Christ's sacrifice of propitiation, passing over and ignoring former sin without punishment.

The Eternal Forgiveness of all our Sin

When Jesus died on the cross and was raised from the dead, He became the complete sacrifice for our sin once and for all. Satisfying the justice of a holy and righteous God once and for all eternity!

The writer of Hebrews says it like this: *For Christ (the Messiah) has not entered into a sanctuary made with [human] hands, only a copy and pattern and type of the true one, but [He has entered] into heaven itself, now to appear in the [very] presence of God on our behalf.*

25 Nor did He [enter into the heavenly sanctuary to] offer Himself regularly again and again, as the high priest enters the [Holy of] Holies every year with blood not his own.

26 For then would He often have had to suffer [over and over again] since the foundation of the world? But as it now is, He has once for all at the consummation and close of the ages appeared to put away and abolish sin by His sacrifice [of Himself] Hebrews 9: 24 – 28

Notice what the writer says in verse 26, "But as it now is..." What he is saying is that this is how it now is, like it or not! This is how things are now because of the finished work of Jesus on the cross! He has once for all people, for all time at the consummation and close of the ages appeared to put away and abolish sin by His sacrifice! Providing total forgiveness and pardon for all humanity's offenses against a holy God!

The writer goes on in verse 27. *And just as it is appointed for [all] men once to die, and after that the [certain] judgment,*

28 Even so it is that Christ, having been offered to take upon Himself and bear as a burden the sins of many once and once for all, will appear a second time, not to carry any burden of sin nor to deal with sin, but to bring to full salvation those who are [eagerly, constantly, and patiently] waiting for and expecting Him. [AMP]

Here in verse 28, he makes it clear that this issue of sin is dealt with so completely and utterly that even though Jesus will come again a second time He will never have to deal with this matter again! It is done and will never be an issue between man and God again.

Jesus fully provided forgiveness and pardon before a holy, and perfect God! Leaving us the liberty to live free from guilt, condemnation, shame and fear! In the kingdom of His son there is complete liberty to live free from guilt, condemnation or fear of death through punishment and the judgment of God for sin.

No More Consciousness of Sin!

The problem that many of us still have is that we have been taught to believe that we should still feel guilty even after we have trusted Jesus to pay for our sin. One of the most awesome powers of the finished work of Jesus Christ is that at the cross God's intent was not only to cleanse us of all our sin, but also to cleanse our consciences of all guilt.

In Hebrews 10: 1-23, the writer continues by giving us some insight into what the results will be if we believe and start living according to the truth of the eternal forgiveness of all our sin.

A. (Vs 1) "Perfect"

1. FOR SINCE the Law has merely a rude outline (foreshadowing) of the good things to come--instead of fully expressing those things-- it can never by offering the same sacrifices continually year after year make perfect those who approach [its altars].

This word "perfect" used here is not about being made perfect in our moral behaviour, but is about being made perfect in the sense of wholeness, soundness and peace! "Completeness" as in being made completely and perfectly innocent!

B. (Vs 2) No Consciousness of Sin

2. For if it were otherwise, would [these sacrifices] not have stopped being offered? Since the worshipers had once for all been cleansed, they would no longer have any guilt or consciousness of sin. (Hebrews 10:1 - 2 AMP)

The writer sets a premise here for what he is going to explain later! He clearly states that if there were a sacrifice that had the ability to take care of sin, and make a man completely and perfectly innocent, there would no longer be any guilt or consciousness of sin! That is as plain as you will ever get it.

C. (Vs 4) "The Blood of Bulls and Goats"

4. *Because the blood of bulls and goats is powerless to take sins away. (Hebrews 10:4 AMP)*

It is clear that the Old Testament system of law and sacrifices could not cleanse us of our sin, but instead gave us a consciousness of sin so we cannot live guilt free!

D. (Vs 12 - 14) A Single Sacrifice for Sin Completely Cleansed & Perfected!

"12. Whereas this One [Christ], after He had offered a single sacrifice for our sins [that shall avail] for all time, sat down at the right hand of God....."

13. For by a single offering He has forever completely cleansed and perfected those who are consecrated and made holy. (Hebrews 10:12 - 14 AMP)

The next 10 verses make his case for the fact that there is now a sacrifice that has taken care of sin, once and once for all eternity, and that by this single sacrifice God has cleansed and perfected every believer (made every believer completely and perfectly innocent)!

If that is true (and it is), then according to verse 2, it is also true that every believer today should on longer have any guilt or consciousness of sin!

E. (Vs 15 - 18) God has no Remembrance of our Sin!

17. He then goes on to say, And their sins and

their lawbreaking I will remember no more.

18. Now where there is absolute remission (forgiveness and cancellation of the penalty) of these [sins and lawbreaking], there is no longer any offering made to atone for sin. (Hebrews 10:18 AMP)

The reason we should have no more consciousness of sin today, is because according to Paul, God has no more remembrance of sin today. Because of the sacrifice of Jesus we have absolute forgiveness and cancellation of the penalty for sin! The blood of Jesus also assures us that we need never make any other sacrifice to atone for our sin and lawbreaking! **No penance, no offerings, no vows or indulgences, no consecrations!**

F. (Vs 22) "Purified Conscience"

22. Let us all come forward and draw near with true (honest and sincere) hearts in unqualified assurance and absolute conviction engendered by faith (by that leaning of the entire human personality on God in absolute trust and confidence in His power, wisdom, and goodness), having our hearts sprinkled and purified from a guilty (evil) conscience and our bodies cleansed with pure water. (Hebrews 10:22 AMP)

The blood of Jesus not only cleansed us of all our sin but also if we fully believe and trust in the power and virtue of the blood of Jesus it will cleanse and rid us of a **guilty conscience.**

The Guarantee

There is a guarantee that accompanies this wonderful truth of the finished work of Jesus on the cross.

8 And he guarantees right up to the end that you will be counted free from all sin and guilt on that day when he returns.

9 God will surely do this for you, for he always does just what he says, and he is the one who invited you into this wonderful friendship with his Son, even Christ our Lord."

(1 Cor 1:8-9) [Living Bible]

Note that this scripture says that God guarantees you and I that because of the finished work of Jesus on the cross two thousand years ago we will be counted free from all sin and all guilt on that day when He returns.

What an absolutely wonderful promise this is to us today. God wants you and I to live our lives free from sin and from guilt. Guilt free living is God's best for His people. Will you accept His guarantee for your life today and start living guilt free?

Seven

TAKE A MULLIGAN!

There have been many times in my life and ministry that I have come to a place were I feel like everything that can go wrong is going wrong and that I'm having a tough time in life. A few years ago I came to the end of the year feeing totally stressed, tired, worn out and to a certain degree disappointed and disillusioned. I know that this is where many people are in their personal or professional lives. Maybe this is where you are today, but I would like you to realize that God is still God, and He has not changed. God is still the same Heb 13:8-9 *Jesus Christ is the same yesterday and today and forever. Do not be carried away by all kinds of strange teachings. It is good for our hearts to be strengthened by grace,* (NIV)

It is very important to note that the writer of Hebrews says that we should not be carried away by all kinds of strange teachings or doctrines. This is especially true concerning false teachings that are propagated in this world and blatant error that has been around for many years. But I also believe that many times when we are struggling with tough times in our lives and things are not working out the way we would want them, these very difficult and sometimes contrary circumstances, and situations seem to try and "carry us away" or "teach us strange things" about God.

The Message Bible says it this way; *"Don't be lured away from Him (God) by the latest speculations about Him".* Today God wants to strengthen us with His grace, mercy and love. God wants us to know that even though everything in our life is subject to change and that things do not always work out the way we would like to have it to be, He is never going to change. He is always the same yesterday, today and forever.

I believe that God wants us all to know that with Him in our lives there is always another chance, or another opportunity for life, no matter what!

Another Chance

In amateur golf there is a term called "Taking a Mulligan". This means is that if you had played a poor stroke, which had not worked out as planned. You could take a "Mulligan" or you can have another chance at playing the same stroke without a penalty. The first time that I heard the term "Mulligan" as a serious golfer, it came as a shock to my system. Golf is a game that is known for its strict code of ethics and adherence to the rules of play that govern the game. As a serious golfer I could not believe that people would take a free stroke without paying the penalty demanded by rules of golf. But yet, there are many people who bend the rules of golf to include a "Mulligan" or two in a social round of golf, much to the disgust of purest like myself.

This is often the same for serious Christians. We tend to find it hard to think or believe that there can be another chance with God, but it is true. With God there always another chance free of the penalty of the past. Many times when we have come to a place where we have exhausted all our options and feel like we have come to the end of our opportunities with God, He is always ready and willing to give us a "Mulligan." This is what Micah the prophet was talking about when he came to the end of the book of Micah. (Mic 7:18-20) *"Where is another God like you, who pardons the sins of the survivors among his people? You cannot stay angry with your people, for you love to be merciful. Once again you will have compassion on us. You will tread our sins beneath your feet; you will throw them into the depths of the ocean! You will bless us as you promised Jacob long ago. You will set your love upon us, as you promised our father Abraham!"* [TLB]

He proclaims, like many of us should when we realize the greatness of our God. "Where is there another God like our God"! All the other gods that are worshiped in the world today cannot be compared with the God of the Bible. Micah tells us why. "Who pardons the sins of the survivors among his people." There is no other God that is willing and able to forgive the sins of the people. What is even more profound is that our God not only is willing and able to forgive our sins. He "cannot stay angry with His people". Micah says "for you LOVE to be merciful". What a wonderful truth to know and believe today. God is merciful. That means that He is always willing, and able to treat us and give us better than we deserve.

Then Micah goes on in verse 19, "Once again you will have compassion on us". Note he said, "once again." That means that God had compassion on them before and He is willing and able to have compassion on them again. Our God is a God of another chance, and another chance, and another chance.

Everyone has a need for another chance

God knows that all of us are going to need another chance somewhere in our walk of life, and this new chance is for all His people.

1. Maybe you have failed miserably in your past, or in the area of morality

or in business, even in the area of relationships. I believe God wants you to know that you can put your past behind you and experience the joy of another chance. After all, the gospel is never about your past. It is always about your future. It is not where you start that counts, it is where you end up that counts.

2. Maybe you have gone through some tragedy or hardship in your the resent past leaving you feeling like God has forsaken you and abandoned you. God wants you to know that no matter what you have experienced, He is for you and will never leave you nor forsake you. (Rom 8:28 – 39) *"And we know that all things work together for good to them that love God, to them who are the called*

according to his purpose". [KJV]

3. Maybe you have felt like your chances have passed you by, and you may feel that maybe you are too old, or you are too tired, or to inadequate, or you just feel like it is too late. God wants you to know that it is never to late! The bible says that "now is the day of salvation" There is never a better time than today to start. It is never to late to start over, and you should never be afraid to start over with God on your side.

4. Maybe this last year you have felt God's calling to do His work, but you have ignored it, or postponed it for too long. Now you feel like have missed the opportunity for God to work through you. God wants you to know that he can and will still

work through you. God never gives up on us. See: (Rom 11:29) *"For God's gifts and His call are irrevocable. [He never withdraws them when once they are given, and He does not change His mind about those to whom He gives His grace or to whom He sends His call.* [AMP]

The People that God used

If you think that God could never use you think again, look at the people God used.

Noah was a drunk

Abraham was too old

Isaac was a daydreamer

Leah was ugly

Joseph was abused

Moses had a stuttering problem

Gideon was afraid

Sampson had long hair and was a womanizer

Rahab was a prostitute

Jeremiah and Timothy were too young

David had an affair and was a murderer

Elijah was suicidal

Isaiah preached naked

Jonah ran from God

Naomi was a widow

Job went bankrupt

John the Baptist ate bugs

Peter denied Christ

The Disciples fell asleep while praying

Martha worried about everything

Mary Magdalene was, well you know

The Samaritan woman was divorced, more than once

Zaccheus was too small
Paul was too religious
Timothy had an ulcer...AND
Lazarus was dead!

Take a Mulligan

I sense that the Spirit of God is saying, "Are you tired, disappointed and frustrated? Then "Take a Mulligan!" with God on your side take another chance at life, or take another chance at your relationships, or your business." I am reminded of a story I once heard about a homeless man begging at a street corner. One day as he was about his business he stopped a rich man who was passing by, to ask him for a spare coin. As the rich man stopped to take out his spare chance he looked at the beggar and realized that he knew the beggar from somewhere. At the same time the beggar recognized the rich man. They had been friends in school. "Do you still remember me from school. We were in the same class together." he said. The rich men instantly remembered him and feeling sorry because his friend had fallen on hard times reached for his checkbook and wrote out a check for $10,000.00 to the homeless man, saying "Take this money and get a new start in life."

Eyes full of tears the homeless man walked to the bank. Stopping at the door he looked in and saw the people in the bank all dressed in good clothing. The bank was so nice and clean with air-conditioning. Looking at himself, his tattered clothes, and his body odor he thought, "I can't go in there and try to cash this check. They will think I have forged it." So he turned around and walked away.

The next day the rich man saw the beggar still standing at the street corner begging, so he asked him,

"Why are you still begging after I gave you that check yesterday?"
The beggar told him what had happened and how he felt about going to the bank.

The rich man said; "Listen my friend, what makes this check good and valid is not your past, your clothes or your appearance but my signature. Go now and cash it, and get a new start in life!"

My friend, God's signature is on your next chance. Jesus died and shed His blood to give you another chance in life. His blood shed for you two thousand years ago is all you need to take another opportunity for life. It is God's forgiveness. That's the only guarantee you need for today, God's forgiveness, love and grace will help you if you will choose to take a Mulligan today.

Eight

MOVE YOUR MAGNIFYING GLASS

I believe it is so important to change what I "think" I see in my circumstances every day. Almost all of us have some reason why we feel our lives are not measuring up and how bad things seem to be.

When we have difficulties we start looking back and wondering about the "what if's". What if I had taken that opportunity or done something differently? What if I hadn't fought with my loved one? What if I won that competition or money? The fact is that we can't know what would have happened if we had done things differently or if they had turned out otherwise. We usually make our choices based on our circumstances at the time.

But these things in our lives don't have to rule our outcome. God says He knows the plans and thoughts He has for us. Thoughts for good and not for evil Lately, I have heard the Lord say over and over: "Move your magnifying glass!" Gradually the Lord got through to me that my focus is off.

We all have a magnifying glass that we look at our lives with. Having a magnifying glass is not the problem. The problem is where it is focused! Very often we focus on the negative stuff in our life. But I believe God wants to challenge us to move the magnifying glass.

Psalms is full of times where David says, "Come magnify the Lord with me and let us exalt his name!" The emphasis is on "magnifying" the Lord and not the things that are happening. What we place our focus on will automatically become bigger and take over our thoughts. Personally I would rather have the Lord become bigger and the problems and other stuff in life diminish!! After all He is greater in us than he who is in the world.

In Matthew 11: 28-30 Jesus says: *"Are you tired? Worn out? Burned out on religion?*

Come to me. Get away with me and you'll recover your life. I'll show you how to take a real rest. Walk with me and work with me – watch how I do it. Learn the unforced rhythms of grace. I won't lay anything heavy or ill-fitting on you. Keep company with me and you'll learn to live freely and lightly" (MSG Bible)

The Ben Campbell Johnson paraphrase says it this way: *Take the burden of responsibility I give you and thereby discover your life and your destiny. I am gentle and humble; I am willing to relate to you and to permit you to learn at your own rate; then, in fellowship with me, you will discover the meaning of your life.*

In John 16:33, Jesus tells us to have courage and be confident in the midst of our trials and frustrations. He declares His victory over the things in this world. The Amplified says, *"I have deprived it (the world) of power to harm you and have conquered it for you."* Imagine that your current frustration is in human form. Now picture this enemy in the desert. Your enemy is not getting a drop of water or a crumb of food. Just so, Jesus has deprived the world of all power to harm you and has conquered it for you.

Sometimes we give our problems a little more power than they deserve. I have noticed in my own life that the minute I begin focusing on what I'm frustrated or worried about, I begin feeding it and building it up. The one thing that always happens is I lose my focus and then I become angry or disappointed and ultimately become weak.

God's love for us NEVER EVER changes. His patience with us never changes. That's the place where we should keep our magnifying glass – on His love and passion for us. I recently found the following saying that really touched my heart.

It's as if God is saying this to me (and you): IF I LOVE YOU AT THE BEGINNING OF OUR JOURNEY (when you get born again) AND PROMISE TO LOVE YOU WHEN WE REACH OUR DESTINATION (eternal life with Him), THEN THERE IS NO REASON TO DOUBT MY LOVE ALONG THE WAY, EVEN IF THE ROAD GETS BUMPY.

I'd like to encourage you to move your magnifying glass. Take time every day and begin to focus on God and His work in your life. His mercies are new EVERY morning. His hopes are FADELESS under ALL circumstances. He is an EVER-PRESENT help in time of trouble. He heaps us with BENEFITS EVERY day.

TAKE IT TO HEART TODAY!

No matter who you are…
No matter where you are…
You matter to God!

Not because of what you do…
Nor what you've ever done…
God loves you because—God is Love!

This is love: not that we loved God, but that He loved us and sent His Son as an atoning sacrifice for our sins" (adapted from 1 John 4:10).

"For God so loved the world that He gave His only begotten Son, that whoever believes in Him should not perish but have everlasting life" (John 3:16).

"Greater love has no one than this, than to lay

down one's life for his friends." Jesus said, "You are My friends" (John 15:13-14).

Jesus has done all the work for you! The work is finished. Jesus did His part. All you need to do is act on it and receive it.

A Brand New Creature

"Therefore, if anyone is in Christ, he is a new creation; old things have passed away; behold, all things have become new" (2 Corinthians 5:17).

Righteous...In Right-Standing With God

"For He made Him who knew no sin to be sin for us, that we might become the righteousness of God in Him" (2 Corinthians 5:21).

Free From Condemnation

"There is therefore now no condemnation to those who are in Christ Jesus" (Romans 8:1).

BECOME A PARTNER AND HELP US SPREAD THE GOSPEL OF PEACE AND GRACE

For further ministry information and products available or if you would like to partner with us to take this message of grace and peace around the world, visit our website at:

www.kingdomlifeministry.com

36518972R00074

Made in the USA
San Bernardino, CA
25 July 2016